Simply Sensational™
Chili Recipes

GOLDEN WEST PUBLISHERS

Cover photo © 1997 Lois Ellen Frank/Westlight

> *Note:* Coarsely ground meats including chuck roasts, hamburger, flank steak and any other kind of beef (or chicken) can be substituted for ground beef in any of the following recipes.

ISBN #1-885590-27-X

Printed in the United States of America

Copyright © 1997 by Bruce and Lee Fischer. All rights reserved. This book or any portion thereof may not be reproduced in any form, except for review purposes, without the written permission of the publisher.

Information in this book is deemed to be authentic and accurate by publisher. However, publisher disclaims any liability incurred in connection with the use of information appearing in this book.

Golden West Publishers, Inc.
4113 N. Longview Ave.
Phoenix, AZ 85014, USA
(602) 265-4392

Table of Contents

Texas Chili	7
Zesty New Mexico Chili	8
Chili Salinas	9
Crockpot Chili	10
Lemon-Wine Chili	11
Roundup Chili	12
Venison Chili	14
West Texas Chili	15
Cincinnati Chili	16
Hot & Spicy Chili	17
Beer Chili	18
Chuckwagon Chili	20
California Chili	21
Hot Chili	22
Mountain Venison Chili	23

Bandito Chili	24
Texas Chili with Beans	25
Red Chili	26
Hearty, Old-Fashioned Chili	27
Bite-the-Bullet Chili	28
Bowl of Fire	30
Ginger Chili	31
Tex-Mex Chili	32
Rio Grande Chili	34
Arizona's Fine Chili	35
Super Chili	36
Sunday Night Chili	37
Hog-Heaven Chili	38
Mexican Chili	39
Old-Fashioned Chili	40
All-American Chili	41
Low-Sodium Chili	42
Easy Chili	43

- Zesty Chili 44
- Chili Rojo 45
- Chili Creole-Style 46
- Lima Bean Chili 47
- Mescalero Chili 48
- Fiesta Chili 49
- Bueno Chili con Carne 50
- Mexican Chili with Beans 51
- One-Pan Chili 52
- Chili Supreme 53
- Spitfire Chili 54
- Arizona Trail Chili 56
- Prospector's Chili 57
- Grandpa's Chili con Carne 58
- Cowboy Chili Beans 59
- Chorizo Chili Beans 60
- Oklahoma Chili 61
- Border Chili 62

Chili is a dish that has become as American as apple pie. Its origins can be traced to the Southwest, where early cowboys may have used native chile peppers for seasoning their stews, thus creating the first "bowl of red." Indians and Mexicans have been cooking and seasoning with chiles for hundreds of years. Modern day chili cookoffs and contests have evolved in more recent times.

Today there are chilis for every taste and every passion. Chilis with beans and chiles without, chilis with spicy heat and milder chilis for the more sensitive. Presented herein are savory delights sure to warm you on a cold winter's day, or to keep your internal fires stoked and your energy levels high. These authentic easy-to-prepare chili recipes will warm your palates and your souls.

Texas Chili

3 lbs. boneless CHUCK ROAST
3 cloves GARLIC, chopped
3 Tbsp. FLOUR
4 to 6 Tbsp. CHILI POWDER

2 tsp. ground CUMIN
1 Tbsp. leaf OREGANO
2 cans BEEF BROTH
SALT and PEPPER to taste

Cut meat into 1" cubes. Sauté in a small amount of oil in a large pot, until brown. Lower heat and stir in garlic. In a small bowl combine flour, chili powder, and cumin. Sprinkle flour mixture over meat and stir until coated on all sides. Crumble oregano over all. Add 1 1/2 cans broth and stir until well blended. Add salt and pepper. Bring to a boil, reduce heat; simmer partially covered over low heat for 1 1/2 hours. Stir occasionally. Add remaining broth, cook 30 minutes more. Cool, cover and refrigerate overnight. Serves 8.

Zesty New Mexico Chili

1/2 cup OIL
3 med. ONIONS, chopped
3 cloves GARLIC, chopped
3 lbs. GROUND BEEF
1 can (16 oz.) crushed TOMATOES
1 can (9 oz.) TOMATO SAUCE
4 Tbsp. ground NEW MEXICO CHILI POWDER
1 tsp. CUMIN POWDER
1 Tbsp. SALT
1/2 tsp. BLACK PEPPER
1 tsp. CAYENNE

Heat oil and sauté onions and garlic until almost brown. Add ground meat and cook until no longer pink. Add tomatoes, tomato sauce and all seasonings. Stir thoroughly. Add water to thin, if needed. Simmer for about an hour. Stir often. Serves 6 to 8.

Chili Salinas

2 Tbsp. OLIVE OIL
2 med. ONIONS, finely chopped
2 or 3 cloves GARLIC, crushed
3 lbs. GROUND CHUCK
1/2 cup chopped BELL PEPPER
1/2 cup chopped CELERY
1 can (4 oz.) diced GREEN CHILES
1 can (28 oz.) TOMATO SAUCE
1 can (28 oz.) stewed TOMATOES, chopped
1 bottle (2 oz.) CHILI POWDER
1/2 tsp. OREGANO
1 tsp. CUMIN
2 tsp. SALT
freshly ground PEPPER

Place oil, onions and garlic in a large pot and sauté. Add meat and cook over medium heat until no longer pink. Add remaining ingredients and bring to a boil. Turn heat to low, cover pot and simmer for at least three hours, stirring occasionally. Add small amounts of hot beef bouillon if too thin. Serves 6.

Crockpot Chili

8 lbs. GROUND BEEF
3 med. ONIONS, chopped
2 BELL PEPPERS, chopped
3 stalks CELERY, chopped
1 can (6 oz.) TOMATO PASTE
2 cans (16 oz. ea.) stewed TOMATOES
2 cans (24 oz. ea.) TOMATO SAUCE
3 cloves GARLIC, chopped
2 bottles (3 oz. ea.) CHILI POWDER
3 Tbsp. SALT
1 can (1 oz.) CHILE SALSA
1 tsp. diced HOT GREEN CHILES
GARLIC SALT
COARSE GROUND PEPPER
OREGANO

Brown beef in large skillet. Remove meat from skillet with a slotted spoon and place in a large crock pot. Add vegetables and all other ingredients. Cook on low heat for three hours. Serves 16.

Lemon-Wine Chili

1 lb. lean GROUND BEEF
1 med. ONION, finely chopped
1 clove GARLIC, minced fine
1 can (28 oz.) stewed TOMATOES
1 cup BURGUNDY WINE
JUICE of large fresh LEMON
4 Tbsp. CHILI POWDER
1 tsp. SEASONED SALT

1/2 tsp. LEMON PEPPER
1/4 tsp. BLACK PEPPER
1/4 tsp. CAYENNE PEPPER
1/2 tsp. HOT DRY MUSTARD
1/2 tsp. CELERY SEED
1/2 tsp. CUMIN
1/4 tsp. OREGANO

Brown beef with onions and garlic, stirring frequently. Add remaining ingredients and simmer for at least one hour. Serves 6.

Roundup Chili

- 3 dry mild RED CHILE PEPPERS
- 4 cups WATER
- 4 lbs. GROUND BEEF
- 1 lg. ONION, finely chopped
- 3 cloves GARLIC, finely chopped
- 3 stalks CELERY, finely chopped
- 1 can (8 oz.) TOMATO SAUCE
- 1 can (4 oz.) diced GREEN CHILES
- 1 Tbsp. ground CUMIN
- 1 Tbsp. whole OREGANO, crumbled
- 1 whole BAY LEAF
- 3 Tbsp. mild CHILI POWDER
- 1/4 tsp. WHITE PEPPER
- 1/2 tsp. BLACK PEPPER
- 1 tsp. PAPRIKA
- 1 cube BEEF BOUILLON
- 1/2 sq. unsweetened CHOCOLATE
- 1 Tbsp. FLOUR
- 3 Tbsp. CORNMEAL
- SALT to taste

Soak peppers in water. When soft, remove to paper towels and reserve water. Grind peppers fine in a meat grinder or food

(Continued next page)

(**Roundup Chili** *continued from previous page*)

processor. In a large pot, brown meat and drain off extra fat. Add onion and garlic to meat and cook for five minutes, stirring occasionally. Add the balance of ingredients except for chocolate, flour, cornmeal and salt. Add the ground chile peppers and the reserved pepper water. Bring mixture to a boil, cover, reduce heat and simmer for one hour, stirring occasionally.

Add chocolate and stir until completely melted. Cover and simmer very slowly for 1/2 hour, stirring occasionally. Mix flour and cornmeal together. Add enough water to make a thin paste and stir into meat mixture. Cook, uncovered, stirring constantly, for five minutes or until slightly thickened. Add salt to taste. Remove bay leaf. Serves 8.

> *This recipe is best when made in a well-seasoned iron pot, but any pot can be used. It freezes very well.*

Venison Chili

2 Tbsp. VEGETABLE OIL
1 lb. VENISON chili meat
1 sm. ONION, grated
1 sm. clove GARLIC, grated
1 tsp. SALT

1 dash CAYENNE PEPPER
3 Tbsp. CHILI POWDER
1/2 tsp. OREGANO
3 cups HOT WATER

Heat oil in a large pot. Add meat and fry until brown. Add onion and garlic and sauté lightly. Add salt, pepper, chili powder and oregano. Stir. Add hot water, cover and bring to a boil. Lower heat and simmer 30 minutes (or until meat is tender). Serves 6 to 8.

West Texas Chili

3 lbs. lean GROUND CHUCK
3 Tbsp. CORN OIL
HOT WATER
3 lg. ONIONS, chopped
3 cloves GARLIC, chopped
1 tsp. OREGANO
1 tsp. ground CUMIN

4 Tbsp. CHILI POWDER
2 tsp. CAYENNE Pepper
1 Tbsp. SUGAR
3 tsp. SALT
2 Tbsp. PAPRIKA
1 can (8 oz.) TOMATO SAUCE
3 Tbsp. MASA HARINA

Put meat into a large cast-iron pot. Add corn oil and sear meat over high heat, stirring constantly until it is no longer pink. Add hot water to just cover meat. Add remaining ingredients (except masa harina), and simmer 2 1/2 hours. Remove all grease from surface of mixture. If too thin, sprinkle in masa harina and stir for 15 more minutes.

Serves 6 to 8.

Cincinnati Chili

- 2 lbs. GROUND BEEF
- 4 med. ONIONS, chopped
- 1 clove GARLIC, minced
- 2 tsp. VINEGAR
- 1 can (12 oz.) TOMATO PASTE
- 2 to 3 Tbsp. CHILI POWDER
- 3 tsp. CINNAMON
- 1 tsp. TABASCO®
- 2 dashes WORCESTERSHIRE SAUCE
- 1 quart WATER
- SALT AND PEPPER
- SPICE BAG*

Sauté beef, onions and garlic. Add all other ingredients. Simmer, partially covered, one hour. Remove spice bag.

Serving suggestion: Serve in layers: Hot spaghetti, ***Cincinnati Chili,*** shredded sharp cheese and chopped onions. Top with oyster crackers.

*Spice Bag: • 4 DRY PEPPERS   • 35 ALLSPICE   • 5 BAY LEAVES

Hot & Spicy Chili

1 lb. GROUND BEEF
2 Tbsp. CHILI POWDER
1 1/2 cloves GARLIC, minced
1 med. ONION, chopped
1/4 tsp. BLACK PEPPER
1/4 tsp. CAYENNE
1 tsp. CUMIN

1 tsp. OREGANO
4 Tbsp. FLOUR
2 cups TOMATO JUICE

Brown beef in a large skillet. Add seasonings and flour and mix well. Stir in tomato juice. Bring chili to a boil, stirring occasionally. Reduce heat and simmer 15 to 20 minutes. Serves 4 to 6.

Beer Chili

8 to 10 strips lean BACON, cubed
4 lbs. very coarsely ground, premium STEW MEAT
3 med. ONIONS, diced
3 stalks CELERY, diced
2 lg. GREEN BELL PEPPERS, diced
3 lg. cloves GARLIC, finely chopped
leftover cooked MEATS (beef, pork, venison, etc. bones OK)
1 cup premium BEER
6 whole CLOVES
6 oz. CHILI POWDER
1 can (6 oz.) TOMATO PASTE
2 cans (28 oz. ea.) and 1 can (16 oz.) TOMATOES

(Continued on next page)

(*Beer Chili* continued from previous page)

1 HOT GREEN CHILE, seeded and diced
1 Tbsp. SALT
1 Tbsp. PAPRIKA
2 lg. BAY LEAVES

In large Dutch oven, cook bacon over medium heat, stirring often, until bacon separates and starts to curl. Add stew meat (excess fat removed), onions, celery, peppers and garlic. Cook until meat browns. Stir often and skim off fat. Add leftover meats, beer, cloves, chili powder and tomato paste. Stir thoroughly. Add tomatoes with liquid, hot green chile, salt and paprika. Stir thoroughly again, breaking up tomatoes with spoon. Add bay leaves. Stir and simmer, covered, four hours. Uncover and simmer another one to two hours. Stir occasionally. Remove any bones and bay leaves. Serves 4.

Chuckwagon Chili

1/2 lb. diced BACON
2 lbs. lean BEEF
1 cup chopped ONION
1 clove GARLIC, minced
1 Tbsp. CIDER VINEGAR

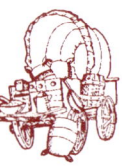

2 cans (15 oz. ea.) TOMATO SAUCE
1 Tbsp. BROWN SUGAR
3 Tbsp. CHILI POWDER
1 cup STUFFED OLIVES

Fry bacon in a large pot until crisp and brown and drain on paper towels. Pour off all but 3 tablespoons drippings. Cut beef into 3/4" cubes and brown (1/3 at a time) in pot; remove and set aside. Fry onion and garlic in same pan. Add beef cubes, tomato sauce, vinegar, sugar and chili powder. Cover and simmer 2 1/2 hours (or until meat is tender), stirring occasionally. Add fried bacon and olives to pot 15 minutes before end of cooking time. Serves 6 to 8.

California Chili

- 2 lbs. GROUND BEEF
- 2 cups chopped ONIONS
- 1 cup diced GREEN BELL PEPPER
- 2 cloves GARLIC, minced
- 1 tsp. each SALT, PAPRIKA, OREGANO and ground CUMIN
- 1/4 cup CHILI POWDER
- 1 to 2 tsp. TABASCO®
- 1 tsp. INSTANT COFFEE
- 1 can (8 oz.) TOMATO SAUCE
- 1 can (16 oz.) TOMATOES
- 1 cup WATER

Break up ground beef in a large heavy saucepan. Add onions, pepper and garlic; cook, stirring frequently, until beef is browned and vegetables are tender. Add balance of ingredients and stir to mix well. Bring to a boil; reduce heat and simmer, uncovered for 45 minutes or until thickened.
Serves 6 to 8.

Hot Chili

1 med. ONION, grated
OIL for sautéing
1 lb. GROUND BEEF
1 clove GARLIC, mashed
Dash of CAYENNE

3 Tbsp. CHILI POWDER
3 Tbsp. FLOUR (or cornstarch)
1 can (16 oz.) TOMATOES
WATER as needed

Heat oil and sauté onion. Add meat and stir until no longer pink. Drain grease thoroughly. Add garlic, cayenne, chili powder and stir well. Add flour (or cornstarch) slowly and stir. Mash tomatoes, add to meat mixture and stir. Add water to cover completely. Simmer for 2 hours, stirring occasionally. Serves 6.

Mountain Venison Chili

2 lbs. boiled VENISON, ground
1 qt. VENISON BROTH (or water)
2 med. ONIONS, finely chopped
1 can (15 oz.) TOMATO SAUCE
1 tsp. ALLSPICE
1 tsp. ground CORIANDER
1 to 2 BAY LEAVES
1/2 tsp. crushed RED PEPPER
1 tsp. ground CUMIN
4 cloves GARLIC, minced
2 Tbsp. RED CIDER VINEGAR
4 Tbsp. CHILI POWDER
2 tsp. SALT
1/2 oz. unsweetened BAKING CHOCOLATE
1 tsp. CINNAMON

In a large pot, combine venison and broth (or water) and stir. Boil slowly for 30 minutes. Add balance of ingredients, stir to blend and bring to a boil. Reduce heat and simmer uncovered for three hours. Cover pot after 2 hours. Remove bay leaves. Serve with bowls of sour cream and chutney on the side.
Serves 6 to 8.

Bandito Chili

4 strips BACON
3 cloves GARLIC
5 lbs. lean, GROUND BEEF
2 lbs. ONIONS, chopped
2 cans (8 oz. ea.) diced
    GREEN CHILES
5 tsp. CHILI POWDER

8 dashes PEPPER SAUCE
1 tsp. OREGANO
1 tsp. CUMIN
2 tsp. SWEET BASIL
3 cans (16 oz. ea.) crushed
    TOMATOES
2 cups RED WINE

Cut bacon into squares, place in bottom of Dutch oven or heavy pot, and heat. Add garlic, beef, onions, chiles, and stir. When mixture has browned, add spices and tomatoes. Add wine, bring to a boil, and simmer for two hours. Makes one gallon of chili.

Texas Chili with Beans

- 1 lb. dried PINTO BEANS
- 3/4 cup SALAD OIL
- 3 lbs. STEW MEAT
- 3 lg. ONIONS, chopped
- 3 cloves GARLIC, minced
- 1/3 cup CHILI POWDER
- 2 tsp. SALT
- 3 tsp. TABASCO®
- 1 tsp. ground CUMIN
- 1 tsp. PAPRIKA
- 1 can (8 oz.) TOMATO SAUCE
- 1 can (6 oz.) TOMATO PASTE
- 1 qt. WATER

Cover beans with water and soak overnight. Drain, place in saucepan and cover generously with cold water. Bring to a boil, cover, reduce heat and simmer two hours. Heat oil in large saucepan and add stew meat, onions and garlic. Cook until meat is browned. Add remaining ingredients; stir to mix well. Bring to a boil and reduce heat. Simmer, uncovered, two hours or until meat is tender. Stir in drained beans before serving.
Serves 8 to 10.

Red Chili

- 2 cups dried PINTO BEANS
- 1 quart WATER
- 1 lb. GROUND CHUCK
- 2 Tbsp. OIL
- 1/2 cup chopped ONIONS
- 1/2 cup KETCHUP
- 1/2 cup WATER
- 1 Tbsp. SALT
- 2 Tbsp. SUGAR
- 2 Tbsp. CHILI POWDER

Soak pinto beans in water overnight. Wash beans twice, cover with water and bring to a full boil. Reduce heat and simmer 1 1/2 hours. Heat oil in a large skillet. Add meat and onions and cook over medium heat, stirring continuously, until meat is no longer pink. Add remaining ingredients and simmer 30 minutes. Combine meat mixture with beans and simmer 30 minutes more. Serves 4 to 6.

Hearty, Old-Fashioned Chili

2 lg. ONIONS, sliced
2 GREEN BELL PEPPERS, chopped
2 lbs. GROUND BEEF
1 can (16 oz.) KIDNEY BEANS
2 cans (8 oz.) seasoned TOMATO SAUCE
2 Tbsp. CHILI POWDER
2 tsp. SALT
dash PAPRIKA and CAYENNE

Brown onion, green pepper and meat in a skillet. In a saucepan, add beans, 1/2 of bean liquid, meat mixture, and remaining ingredients. Stir, cover and simmer 1 1/2 hours stirring occasionally. Serves 8 to 10.

Bite-the-Bullet Chili

1/3 lb. PINTO BEANS
1/3 lb. KIDNEY BEANS
1/3 lb. RED or PINK BEANS
OLIVE OIL
1 lb. CHUCK, cubed
2 ONIONS, chopped
4 cloves GARLIC, crushed
1/2 GREEN BELL PEPPER, chopped
1/3 lb. MUSHROOMS, chopped
1 lg. stalk CELERY, chopped
3 cans (14 1/2 oz. ea.) ITALIAN STEWED TOMATOES
1/4 cup chopped fresh BASIL
1/4 cup chopped fresh PARSLEY
4 Tbsp. CHILI POWDER
3 Tbsp. CUMIN
1 Tbsp. OREGANO
1 tsp. CAYENNE
1 Tbsp. MARJORAM
1 Tbsp. SUGAR
2 cans (8 oz. ea.) TOMATO PASTE
SALT to taste

(Continued on next page)

*(**Bite-the-Bullet Chili** continued from previous page)*

Combine beans in a large pan, cover with water and soak overnight. Rinse beans and set aside. In a large Dutch oven, heat oil and brown meat, onions, garlic, green pepper, mushrooms and celery until meat is no longer pink. Add beans to meat mixture. Crush Italian tomatoes.* Add tomatoes, spices and water (if needed) to barely cover mixture. Simmer for at least one hour or until meat is tender. Remove from heat and stir in tomato paste. Correct seasonings to taste.

*Use hands or electric beater to crush seasonings. Seeds of Italian tomatoes should not be broken as they may turn chili bitter. Adding tomato paste after removing from heat also prevents chili from becoming bitter.

Bowl of Fire

2 lbs. dried RED BEANS
3 lbs. GROUND BEEF
1/4 cup OLIVE OIL
1 1/2 qts. WATER
6 Tbsp. CHILI POWDER
3 tsp. SALT
10 cloves GARLIC, chopped fine
1 tsp. ground CUMIN

1 tsp. OREGANO
1 tsp. RED PEPPER
1 Tbsp. SUGAR
3 Tbsp. PAPRIKA
3 Tbsp. FLOUR
6 Tbsp. CORN MEAL
1 cup WATER

Cover beans with water and soak overnight. Boil beans until tender and drain. Braise meat in olive oil until brown. Add water; simmer 1 1/2 hours. Add next 8 ingredients. Simmer 30 minutes then increase heat until bubbling. Combine flour and cornmeal with water and stir into chili mixture. Cook for five more minutes, stirring constantly. Serves 12.

Ginger Chili

- 1 Tbsp. CIDER VINEGAR
- 2 Tbsp. WATER
- 4 (2") GINGER COOKIES
- 2 Tbsp. OIL
- 1 lb. GROUND BEEF
- 1/2 lb. lean GROUND PORK
- 1 1/2 cups chopped ONION
- 1 cup diced CELERY
- 1 lg. clove GARLIC, minced
- 1 med. GREEN BELL PEPPER, chopped
- 1 can (16 oz.) diced TOMATOES
- 1 to 2 Tbsp. CHILI POWDER
- 2 tsp. SALT
- 1 tsp. SUGAR
- 2 cans (15 oz. ea.) RED KIDNEY BEANS, drained

Combine vinegar, water and ginger cookies. Place oil and meats in a large skillet; stir and cook until lightly browned. Add onion, celery, garlic, and peppers. Cook and stir until onions are golden. Add cookie mixture, tomatoes, chili powder, salt and sugar. Bring to a boil, reduce heat, cover, and simmer for one hour. Add beans and heat thoroughly. Serves 8.

Tex-Mex Chili

3 1/2 lbs. lean boneless CHUCK ROAST, cut into 1/2" cubes
3 Tbsp. OIL
3 cloves GARLIC, minced
1 tsp. crushed, dry RED PEPPERS
6 Tbsp. CHILI POWDER
1 1/2 tsp. CUMIN SEEDS
3 Tbsp. MASA HARINA
1 Tbsp. leaf OREGANO
2 tsp. SALT
1/2 tsp. coarsely ground BLACK PEPPER
1 can (14 1/2 oz.) BEEF BROTH
1 can (8 oz.) TOMATO SAUCE
1 can (2 oz.) CHILI SALSA
3 cups cooked PINTO BEANS
Sharp CHEDDAR CHEESE, grated

In a Dutch oven, add the beef cubes and oil. Stir to coat on all sides and heat over medium heat until meat is no longer pink.

(Continued on next page)

 ***Chili*** *continued from previous page)*

Stir in garlic and red peppers. Remove from heat. In a small bowl, combine chili powder, cumin, masa, oregano, salt and black pepper and sprinkle over beef mixture. Slowly add broth and tomato sauce, stirring until well blended. Return to heat, bringing almost to a boil. Reduce heat to low and cover and simmer 1 1/2 hours. Stir occasionally. Add chili salsa and drained beans and simmer 30 minutes more. Serve in heated bowls, garnished with grated cheese. Serves 6 to 8.

Rio Grande Chili

2 Tbsp. OIL
1 med. ONION, chopped
1 clove GARLIC, crushed
1 lb. GROUND BEEF
2 tsp. SALT
1 tsp. PAPRIKA
2 tsp. CHILI POWDER

2 cans (15 oz. ea.) KIDNEY BEANS
1/2 cup BEAN LIQUID
1 can (16 oz.) stewed TOMATOES
1 can (6 oz.) TOMATO PASTE
1/2 tsp. SUGAR
3/4 tsp. TABASCO®
1 can (15 oz.) whole kernel CORN

Heat oil in large skillet and sauté onion and garlic. Add crumbled beef. Sprinkle meat with salt, paprika and chili powder. Stir and cook until brown Stir in 1/2 cup of liquid from beans (discard the rest). Add tomatoes, tomato paste, sugar and Tabasco. Cover and simmer 30 minutes. Add beans and corn; simmer 15 minutes longer, stirring occasionally. Serves 6.

Arizona's Fine Chili

1 lb. GROUND BEEF
2 cups chopped ONION
1 can (6 oz.) TOMATO PURÉE
1 lb. PINTO BEANS*

3 Tbsp. CHILI POWDER
SALT to taste
1 Tbsp. CUMIN
WATER

In a skillet, cook beef until no longer pink. Drain off excess fat. Add onions, tomato purée and beans. Combine chili powder, salt and cumin and add to mixture. Bring to a boil, turn down heat and cook slowly until onions and beans are tender. Add water if necessary for desired consistency. Serves 4.

*Beans can be soaked overnight, drained and rinsed, or, if added dry, chili must be cooked long enough for beans to tenderize.

Super Chili

- 2 lbs. lean GROUND BEEF
- 1 med. ONION, diced
- 1/4 cup FLOUR
- 1/4 cup CHILI POWDER
- 2 qts. WATER
- 1/2 Tbsp. SALT
- 1/2 Tbsp. PEPPER
- 3/4 tsp. GARLIC POWDER
- 1 tsp. OREGANO
- 1/2 tsp. whole CUMIN
- 1/4 tsp. ground CUMIN
- 4 dashes SEASONED SALT
- 2 cans (14 1/2 oz. ea.) TOMATOES & GREEN CHILES
- 1 can (4 oz.) diced GREEN CHILES
- 2 cups cooked PINTO BEANS

In a large pot, brown meat with onion. Pour off all grease except 1/2 cup. Add flour and chile powder. Stir and cook for one minute. Add two quarts water and bring to boiling point. Add remaining ingredients including undrained, cooked beans. Cover and simmer for one hour. Makes 4 1/2 quarts.

Sunday Night Chili

- 1 cup chopped ONION
- 1 tsp. chopped GARLIC
- 1 1/2 lbs. GROUND BEEF
- 3/4 lb. fresh MUSHROOMS, sliced
- 1 tsp. SALT
- 2 Tbsp. CHILI POWDER
- 1/4 cup WATER
- 1/2 cup KETCHUP
- 2 cans BEEF BROTH
- 2 Tbsp. CORN STARCH
- 1 can (15 oz.) KIDNEY BEANS

In a skillet, fry onion, garlic and ground beef until no longer pink. Drain off excess fat. Add mushrooms and salt and cook for five minutes. Blend chili powder with two tablespoons water. Add chili powder mixture, ketchup and broth to meat and heat to boiling. Blend cornstarch with remaining water and add to meat mixture. Simmer for 15 minutes. Add undrained beans and simmer 10 minutes more. Serves 6.

Hog-Heaven Chili

- 1 lb. GROUND BEEF
- 1/2 lb. HOT PORK SAUSAGE
- 1 lg. ONION, chopped
- 1 clove GARLIC, sliced
- 1 can (12 oz.) TOMATO PASTE
- 1 can (14 1/2 oz.) TOMATOES and CHILES
- 1 can (16 oz.) stewed TOMATOES
- 1 can (15 oz.) PINTO BEANS
- 2 cans (15 oz. ea.) KIDNEY BEANS
- 2 cups WATER
- 1 Tbsp. CHILI POWDER
- 1/2 Tbsp. CUMIN
- 2 tsp. SALT
- 2 Tbsp. SUGAR
- 2 Tbsp. WHITE VINEGAR
- dash of PEPPER

In a heavy skillet, brown beef, sausage, onion and garlic until brown. Drain excess grease and place mixture in a large pot. Add remaining ingredients. Bring to a boil, stirring often; simmer for three hours. Serves 12.

Mexican Chili

- 2 Tbsp. OIL
- 1 lb. GROUND BEEF
- 1 ONION, chopped
- 1/2 GREEN BELL PEPPER, chopped
- 1 can (28 oz.) TOMATOES
- 2 cans (16 oz. ea.) KIDNEY BEANS
- 2 yellow CHILE PEPPERS
- 2 JALAPEÑO PEPPERS
- 1/2 cup WATER
- 3 Tbsp. FLOUR
- 1/4 tsp. GARLIC POWDER
- 1/2 tsp. CUMIN
- 1 tsp. OREGANO
- 1 tsp. SOY SAUCE
- 2 tsp. CHILI POWDER
- 2 tsp. BROWN SUGAR
- 1 Tbsp. SALT

Heat oil in large skillet and add beef, onion, and green bell pepper. Cook until meat is browned. Add tomatoes and beans. Dice peppers and combine thoroughly with water and flour. Add pepper mixture and balance of ingredients to meat mixture and simmer for 30 minutes. Serves 4.

Old-Fashioned Chili

**2 lbs. GROUND BEEF
2 med. ONIONS, chopped
1 clove GARLIC, chopped
1 can (14 1/2 oz.) TOMATOES
3 Tbsp. CHILI POWDER**

**dash RED PEPPER
SALT to taste
1 can (6 oz.) TOMATO PASTE
6 oz. WATER
2 cups cooked PINTO BEANS**

In a heavy skillet, combine meat, onion and garlic. Stir and cook until meat is no longer pink. Pour off all grease. Add tomatoes (including juice), chili powder, red pepper and salt. Simmer one hour. Add tomato paste mixed with water. Simmer another hour, stirring often. Stir in cooked pinto beans and heat thoroughly. Serves 8.

All-American Chili

2 lbs. GROUND BEEF
1 lg. ONION, chopped
2 cloves GARLIC, minced
3 to 5 Tbsp. CHILI POWDER
1 tsp. SALT
1 tsp. dried leaf OREGANO
1 to 2 tsp. TABASCO®
1 can (16 oz.) TOMATOES
1 can (8 oz.) TOMATO SAUCE
1 cup WATER
2 cans (15 oz. ea.) RED KIDNEY BEANS, drained

Break up ground beef in a large saucepan and add onion and garlic. Cook, stirring frequently, until beef is uniformly brown and vegetables are tender. Add remaining ingredients and mix well. Bring to a boil; reduce heat. Simmer, uncovered, 45 minutes, stirring occasionally. Serves 6 to 8.

Low-Sodium Chili

1 lb. DRY BEANS
2 to 3 Tbsp. OIL
1 lb. BEEF HEART
1 lb. lean BEEF CHUCK
1 lg. ONION, chopped
2 lg. cloves GARLIC, minced
1 cup diced CELERY

2 Tbsp. CHILI POWDER
1 tsp. TURMERIC
1 tsp. MARJORAM
1 Tbsp. instant decaf COFFEE
1/2 tsp. NUTMEG
1/2 tsp. OREGANO
1 can (10 1/2 oz.) TOMATO PURÉE

Cover beans with water and soak overnight. Add undrained beans and one tablespoon oil to a saucepan. Simmer until almost tender. Cut semi-frozen meat into 3/4" cubes and dredge with flour. Heat remaining oil in skillet and brown meat cubes with onion, garlic and celery. Add balance of ingredients and simmer one hour. Combine mixtures and simmer 40 to 50 minutes. Serves 6 to 8.

Easy Chili

1 lb. GROUND BEEF
1 cup chopped ONION
1 can (15 oz.) KIDNEY BEANS
1 can (8 oz.) TOMATO SAUCE
1/8 tsp. CAYENNE

2 Tbsp. HOT TACO SAUCE
3/4 tsp. SALT
2 JALAPEÑO PEPPERS*,
 seeded

Brown ground beef and onion in large iron skillet. Add kidney beans (drained), and remaining ingredients (see below). Cover and simmer 1 to 1 1/2 hours.

*If including jalapeño peppers, omit cayenne and hot taco sauce. For a milder chile, use only one jalapeño.

Zesty Chili

- 1 lg. ONION, chopped
- 1/4 cup MARGARINE
- 1 1/2 lbs. GROUND BEEF
- 3 Tbsp. CHILI POWDER
- 1/4 tsp. GARLIC POWDER
- 1/2 tsp. ground CORIANDER
- 1 tsp. CUMIN
- 2 sm. RED CHILE PEPPERS, crushed
- 2 BAY LEAVES
- 1/2 tsp. SALT
- 1/4 tsp. PEPPER
- 1 can (30 oz.) RED BEANS
- 1 can (28 oz.) crushed TOMATOES
- 3 Tbsp. FLOUR
- 1/4 cup cold WATER

In a skillet, sauté onion in margarine and set aside. Add meat to skillet and brown lightly. Drain excess fat. Add onions, spices, beans and tomatoes. Mix flour with water and add to chili. Simmer on low heat one to two hours. Remove bay leaves.

Serves 6 to 8.

Chili Rojo

(Red Chili)

1 lb. lean BEEF CHUCK
   cut to 1/2" cubes
1 Tbsp. OIL
1 med. clove GARLIC, minced
1 med ONION, chopped
1 can (6 oz.) TOMATO PASTE
1 tsp. SALT
1 Tbsp. PAPRIKA
1 can (7 oz.) diced GREEN
   CHILES
1 can (10 1/2 oz.) condensed
   ONION SOUP
1 can (16 oz.) PINTO BEANS
1/4 tsp. ground CUMIN
1 cup WATER

In a large skillet, brown beef in oil. Stir in remaining ingredients. Simmer, covered, 1 1/2 hours. Serves 4 to 6.

Chili Creole-Style

6 Tbsp. BUTTER
5 med. ONIONS, chopped
3 lbs. GROUND BEEF
2 Tbsp. CHILI POWDER
1 Tbsp. SALT
1 tsp. PAPRIKA
3/4 tsp. TABASCO®
3 cans (16 oz. ea.) TOMATOES
1 can (8 oz.) TOMATO SAUCE
1 can (6 oz.) TOMATO PASTE
4 cans (15 oz. ea.) KIDNEY BEANS

Melt butter in a 6-quart saucepan and sauté onion. Add beef; sprinkle with chili powder, salt, paprika and Tabasco. Stir and cook until meat is brown. Add tomatoes, tomato sauce and tomato paste. Cover and simmer 45 minutes. Add beans and heat thoroughly. Serves 12.

Lima Bean Chili

1 cup dry BABY LIMA BEANS
3 cups boiling WATER
2 strips BACON
1/4 cup chopped ONION
1 cup chopped CELERY
1 clove GARLIC

1/2 lb. GROUND BEEF
2 Tbsp. FLOUR
1 tsp. CHILI POWDER
SALT and PEPPER to taste
1/2 cup WATER
1 can (6 oz.) TOMATO PASTE

Combine beans and water and simmer for two hours. In a large skillet fry bacon until nearly crisp. Remove bacon; sauté onion, celery and garlic in drippings. Remove garlic. Push vegetables aside, add crumbled beef and cook until brown. In a bowl, combine flour, chili powder, salt, pepper and water to form a smooth paste. Blend in tomato paste; add mixture to skillet, stirring well. Add undrained beans and stir. Cover and simmer over very low heat for one hour or until lima beans are tender.
Serves 4 to 6.

Mescalero Chili

- 1 lb. DRY BEANS
- 3 lb. CHUCK ROAST
- 2 to 3 lb. HAM BUTT
- 1 1/2 lbs. GROUND BEEF
- 1/2 lb. ITALIAN SAUSAGE
- 1 ONION, chopped
- 2 cloves GARLIC, chopped
- 1 GREEN BELL PEPPER, chopped
- 2 JALAPEÑO PEPPERS, chopped
- 1 can (15 oz.), TOMATO SAUCE
- 1 can (16 oz.) stewed TOMATOES
- SALT and PEPPER to taste

Cover beans with water and soak. In a Dutch oven, add meat with water to cover. Bring to a boil. Add balance of ingredients (except beans) and simmer until meat falls away from bones. Add beans and 1 cup bean water. Simmer until beans are tender. Transfer to a baking dish, sprinkle with grated **cheese**, and bake at 325° for 20 minutes. Serves 6 to 10.

Fiesta Chili

8 slices BACON
1 lb. ITALIAN SAUSAGE, sliced
1 lb. GROUND CHUCK
2 med. ONIONS, chopped fine
4 GREEN ONIONS, chopped fine
4 cloves GARLIC, crushed
2 cans (8 oz. ea.) TOMATO SAUCE
1 can (28 oz.) crushed TOMATOES
2 cans (15 oz. ea.) KIDNEY BEANS
3 JALAPEÑOS, chopped fine
2 tsp. CUMIN
2 tsp. OREGANO
2 tsp. BASIL
SALT to taste

In a large skillet, fry bacon until crisp and set aside. Drain all but one tablespoon bacon drippings from pan and fry Italian sausage, ground chuck, onions and garlic until brown. Drain. Crumble bacon and add to meat mixture along with remaining ingredients. Simmer for 30 minutes. Serves 6 to 8

Bueno Chili con Carne

2 Tbsp. OIL
3 med. ONIONS, chopped fine
2 med. GREEN BELL PEPPERS, chopped fine
1 can (4 oz.) diced GREEN CHILES
2 Tbsp. CHILI POWDER
2 Tbsp. CUMIN
SALT and PEPPER to taste
3 lbs. GROUND BEEF
3 cans (15 oz. ea.) dark red KIDNEY BEANS
2 cans (28 oz. ea.) Italian style TOMATOES

Heat oil in a skillet and sauté onions, peppers, and chiles. Add chili powder, cumin, salt and pepper, and ground beef. Cook until beef is brown. Add kidney beans and tomatoes to skillet. Cover and simmer, stirring occasionally, for eight hours. Serves 8.

Mexican Chili with Beans

- 2 cups PINTO BEANS
- 7 cups WATER
- 2 tsp. SALT
- 1 lb. lean GROUND BEEF
- 1/2 lb. BEEF CHORIZO
- 1 clove GARLIC, chopped
- 1/2 cup chopped ONION
- 1/2 cup fine diced CELERY
- 1 Tbsp. CHILI POWDER
- 3 Tbsp. FLOUR

Wash beans. In a large pot, add beans and water. Cook over low heat for 2 1/2 hours. Add salt and cook 30 minutes more. Fry meat in skillet and drain off excess fat. Add chorizo (Mexican sausage), and fry until it separates. Add garlic, onions, celery and chili powder. Stir-fry for one minute; add flour and stir-fry for another minute. Add meat mixture to beans and simmer for 30 minutes, stirring occasionally. Serves 10 to 12.

One-Pan Chili

1 lb. GROUND BEEF
1 can (46 oz.) TOMATO JUICE
1 lg. ONION, chopped
1 Tbsp. SALT
1/2 tsp. CHILI POWDER
1 can (20 oz.) light KIDNEY BEANS

In a large bowl, mix ground beef and tomato juice together with hands. Add onion, salt, chili powder and beans and mix again. Put mixture into large, heavy pot and simmer two hours. Serves 4 to 6.

Chili Supreme

- 2 Tbsp. OIL
- 3 cloves GARLIC, minced
- 3 lbs. GROUND ROUND STEAK
- 1 lg. ONION, chopped
- 1 lg. GREEN BELL PEPPER, chopped
- 1 stalk CELERY, chopped
- 3 cans (16 oz. ea.) red KIDNEY BEANS
- 1 can (6 oz.) TOMATO PASTE
- 1 can (16 oz.) stewed TOMATOES
- 2 cans (15 oz. ea.) TOMATO SAUCE
- 4 tsp. CHILI POWDER
- 4 BAY LEAVES
- 1 Tbsp. SALT
- 1 (2") hot GREEN CHILE
- 1 oz. CHILI SALSA
- 1 dash CAYENNE
- 1 dash OREGANO
- 12 oz. BEER
- 1/2 cup MASA HARINA
- 1 dash GARLIC SALT
- 1 dash coarsely ground PEPPER

Sauté garlic in oil in a large skillet. Add meat and brown evenly. Pour 1/2 cup drippings into another skillet and sauté onions, pepper and celery. Combine all ingredients in a large pan. Cover and cook over low heat for two hours. Remove bay leaves. Serves 12.

Spitfire Chili

- 1 lb. PINTO BEANS
- 1 sm. jar COCKTAIL ONIONS
- 1/2 lb. SLAB BACON cut into 1" cubes
- 3/4 tsp. THYME
- 1 1/4 tsp. toasted CUMIN
- 4 Tbsp. pure CHILI POWDER
- 1 1/2 cups TOMATO PASTE
- 1 1/2 cups diced ROMA TOMATOES
- 1/4 cup VODKA
- 3 Tbsp. fresh LIME JUICE
- 1 Tbsp. SUGAR
- 1 tsp. SALT
- 1/2 tsp. seasoned PEPPER

Cover beans with water and soak overnight. Drain, add fresh water to cover and liquid from onions (reserving two tablespoons). Bring to a boil and cook until beans are just tender. Drain and set aside. Brown bacon cubes in a skillet and remove. Add onions, thyme, cumin, chili powder, tomato paste, tomatoes

(Continued on next page)

(**Spitfire Chili** continued from previous page)

and reserved onion juice to skillet and heat thoroughly. Blend mixture with beans and place in a baking dish.

Pour vodka* and lime juice over meat and bean mixture and sprinkle sugar, salt and seasoned pepper over all. Arrange bacon cubes on top. Cover dish and bake for one hour in preheated 350° oven. Add more liquid if necessary. Serves 6 to 8.

*One vodka gimlet may be used in lieu of vodka and lime juice.

Arizona Trail Chili

2 cans (15 oz. ea.) RANCH STYLE BEANS
1 oz. ground CUMIN
2 oz. CHILI POWDER
1/2 oz. ground CHILI PEPPER
1 lb. GROUND CHUCK

In a heavy pot, combine pinto beans with ground cumin, chili powder and chili pepper. Bring to a simmer and stir thoroughly. In a skillet, fry meat until no longer pink. Add meat to beanpot and simmer for one hour, stirring occasionally. Serves 2 to 4.

Prospector's Chili

- 1 lb. PINK BEANS
- 3 qts. WATER
- 1 ctn. (11 oz.) CHILI PURÉE
- 1 Tbsp. OIL
- 1 lb. GROUND BEEF
- 1 ONION, chopped
- 1/2 clove GARLIC
- 1 tsp. CHILI POWDER
- 1 tsp. FLOUR
- 1/2 tsp. BLACK PEPPER
- 1 can (15 oz.) TOMATO SAUCE
- 2 cups WATER

Place washed beans in a large pot with water. Add chili purée; cook for 30 minutes over medium heat. Heat oil in a skillet, add meat, onions and garlic. Cook, stirring frequently, until beef is brown. Add chili powder, flour and pepper and stir. Gradually add tomato sauce and water and cook over medium heat for 10 minutes, stirring often. Add meat mixture to beans and cook over low heat for 1 1/2 to 2 hours. Serves 8.

Grandpa's Chili con Carne

2 lbs. GROUND BEEF
SALT and PEPPER
GARLIC SALT
MARGARINE
1 cup chopped CELERY
3 cans (16 oz. ea.) TOMATOES
2 cans (6 oz. ea.) TOMATO PASTE
2 Tbsp. SUGAR
1 can (16 oz.) PINTO BEANS
1 Tbsp. SALT
1 can (4 1/4 oz.) OLIVES
dash of OREGANO
1/2 cup chopped PARSLEY
1 Tbsp. WORCESTERSHIRE
3 Tbsp. CHILI POWDER
1/2 cup chopped ONION
TABASCO® to taste
BAY LEAF, (remove before serving)

Sprinkle beef with salt, pepper and garlic salt. In a skillet, add margarine, beef and celery and cook until meat is brown. Cover and simmer 10 minutes. Add balance of ingredients and simmer 5 to 10 minutes. Serves 8.

Cowboy Chili Beans

2 lbs. RED or PINK BEANS
1 Tbsp. BAKING SODA
3 Tbsp. BACON FAT
1 lg. ONION, chopped
1 GREEN BELL PEPPER, chopped
1 TOMATO, chopped
1 lb. GROUND BEEF
1 can (15 oz.) TOMATO SAUCE
2 BAY LEAVES
1 Tbsp. OREGANO
CHILI POWDER to taste
SALT to taste
1/4 lb. SALT PORK, cut into 3/4" cubes
1 can BEER

Cover beans with water, add baking soda and soak overnight. Drain, wash, and place in a 5-quart, heavy pot. Add water (about 3" over beans). Cook three hours, or until tender. In a skillet, sauté onion, pepper and tomato in bacon fat. Add ground beef and simmer for 1/2 hour. Add tomato sauce and simmer another 1/2 hour. Add meat mixture, beans and rest of ingredients and simmer for two hours. Remove bay leaves. Serves 6.

Chorizo Chili Beans

1 lb. PINTO BEANS
1 lb. MEXICAN SAUSAGE (Chorizo)
1 lb. GROUND BEEF

Wash beans and place in a large pot. Cover with 3" of water and simmer for 1 1/2 hours. Add crumbled sausage and ground beef and cook for an additional hour.

Oklahoma Chili

- 6 lbs. GROUND BEEF
- 2 lbs. GROUND PORK
- 2 oz. PAPRIKA
- 4 lg. ONIONS, chopped
- 1 clove GARLIC, minced
- 3 cans (16 oz. ea.) WHOLE TOMATOES
- 1/2 tsp. BLACK PEPPER
- 1 tsp. SAVOR SALT
- 2 oz. CHILI POWDER
- 1/2 tsp. OREGANO
- 1 oz. CUMIN
- 3 JALAPEÑOS, chopped

Brown meat with paprika. Drain fat and sauté onions and garlic in separate pan. Combine with meat and add remaining ingredients. Cook slowly over low heat for three hours. Serves 8 to 10.

Border Chili

- 3 lbs. GROUND BEEF
- 1 can (15 oz.) TOMATO SAUCE
- 2 cups WATER
- 1 tsp. TABASCO®
- 3 Tbsp. PURE CHILI POWDER
- 1 Tbsp. OREGANO
- 1 tsp. CUMIN
- 2 ONIONS, chopped
- GARLIC to taste
- 1 tsp. SALT
- 1 tsp. CAYENNE
- 1 tsp. PAPRIKA
- 2 JALAPEÑOS, diced
- 4 dried ANCHO CHILES, diced
- 3 tsp. FLOUR

In a large skillet, cook meat until no longer pink. Add tomato sauce, one cup of water, and balance of ingredients except flour. Simmer for 1 hour. Combine flour and remaining cup of water and add to meat mixture. Simmer an additional 45 minutes.

Serves 6 to 8.

Simply Sensational™ Cook Books

GOLDEN WEST PUBLISHERS

"Mini-sized" cookbooks packed with savory recipes! Give your tastebuds a treat with authentic recipes that are both flavorful and easy to make. These books are great for personal use and make wonderful gifts!

Each attractive 5 1/2" x 4" book has 64 pages and is comb bound for lay flat use. All books only $4.95 each!

Simply Sensational™ **SALSA RECIPES**

Simply Sensational™ **BARBECUE RECIPES**

Simply Sensational™ **CHILI RECIPES**

Simply Sensational™ **MEXICAN RECIPES**

For a free catalog of Golden West cookbooks call 1-800-658-5830

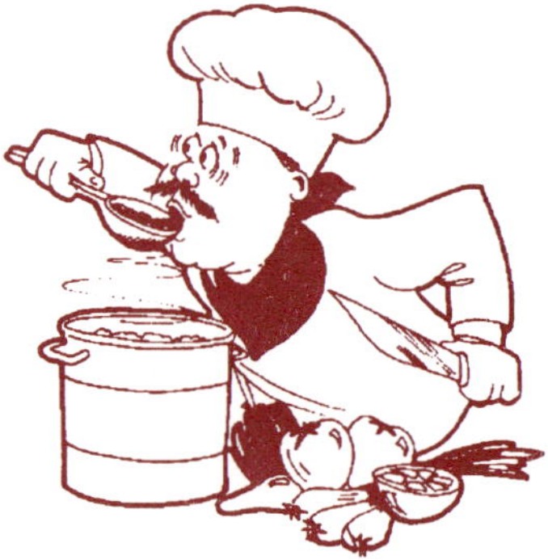

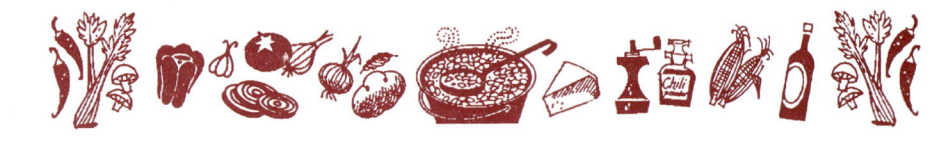